ANIMATED ORIGAMI FACES

JOEL STERN

Photographs by
DAVID GREENFIELD

DOVER PUBLICATIONS, INC.
Mineola, New York

Acknowledgements

This book could not have been produced without the help of the following people:

To my nephew Harry Chiel – for being the "model" folder, and for your terrific suggestions

To Florence Temko – for your continuing counsel and friendship

To Gay Merrill Gross – for your thoughtful editing of words and diagrams

To David Greenfield – for the beautiful photographs of the models

To Kostya Vints – for your extraordinary design talents

To Jamie Chiel, Lisa Kaplan, and Jim Stern – for test-folding the models and for your constructive suggestions

To Ariel Albornoz, John Andrisan, Dorothy Engleman, Miri Golan, Sharon Hearn, Paul Jackson, Leslie Lawson, and Edmon Rodman – for your support and advice along the way

To Norman and Lela Jacoby, and Bates and Petty Metson – for your ongoing encouragement

To my children Rena, Ethan, and Anna – for encouraging me to "Live, Love, Fold!"

And finally, to my wife Susan – for your constant love and support

Bibliographical Note

Animated Origami Faces is a new work, first published by Dover Publications, Inc., in 2007.

Library of Congress Cataloging-in-Publication Data

Stern, Joel, 1953–
  Animated origami faces / Joel Stern ; photographs by David Greenfield.
    p. cm.
  ISBN 13: 978-0-486-46174-8
  ISBN 10: 0-486-46174-2
  1. Origami. 2. Face in art. I. Title.
  TT870.S726 2007
  736'.982—dc22

                                                                2007015032

Manufactured in the United States of America
Dover Publications, Inc., 31 East 2nd Street, Mineola, New York 11501

Contents

Introduction. 4

Symbols 5

Section 1: Models with Mouths and Eyes that Open and Shut 6

    Talking Bird. 7
    Masked Super Hero 10
    Blowfish 13
    Singer 16
    Choir 19
    African Mask 20

Section 2: Models with Jaws that Snap and Ears that Pop Out . . . 23

    Elephant 24
    Panda or Bear. 27
    Dog. 31
    Baboon 35
    Wolf 39
    Monkey 43

Tips for Creating Your Own Models 47

Additional Resources 48

Introduction

Welcome to **Animated Origami Faces**, a book that brings together origami, the art of paperfolding, and animation. With origami, the magic comes from making something out of almost nothing – by simply folding a piece of paper. With animation, the magic comes from creating the illusion of life. This book uses origami techniques to construct human and animal faces that not only talk when you open and close the model, but also blink their eyes and snap their jaws!

The models in this book are different from traditional origami in a number of ways. Origami is usually made from paper that is square and colored on one side. The models here all use American letter-size paper (8½ x 11 inches), which is the same color on both sides. (If you don't live in the U.S. and only have A4-sized paper, you can trim your paper to letter proportions by cutting off 1 inch or 25 millimeters from the bottom.) Most origami models are considered finished when the folding is complete. This book encourages you to color in eyes and other facial features on the folded model.

There are two styles of animated models presented here –

Section 1:   Those with mouths and eyes that open and shut

Section 2:   Those with jaws that snap and ears that pop out

Each section begins with some basic principles of construction and tips for success; at the back you'll find suggestions for taking the next steps on your own.

Within each section the models are ordered by level of difficulty. Make sure you review the diagramming symbols described on the next page, and fold patiently and accurately, always checking the next step to see the result of the move. If your results don't match the picture, don't be discouraged. Set the model aside and try again later. With each attempt, you'll get closer to the goal.

After practicing on letter-size paper, you might also want to try folding these models with paper of different sizes and weights, using the same proportions as 8½ x 11 (about 1:1.3). The models in Section 2 can even be worn as masks if you start with a larger piece of paper.

Check out the *Additional Resources* section in the back for suggested books and web sites, sources for origami paper, and origami organizations.

I hope you enjoy folding the models in this book and, even more, creating your own!

Symbols

The origami symbols used in this book are standard throughout the world. You'll find that as you become accustomed to working with them, you'll be able to read the diagrams without referring to the words.

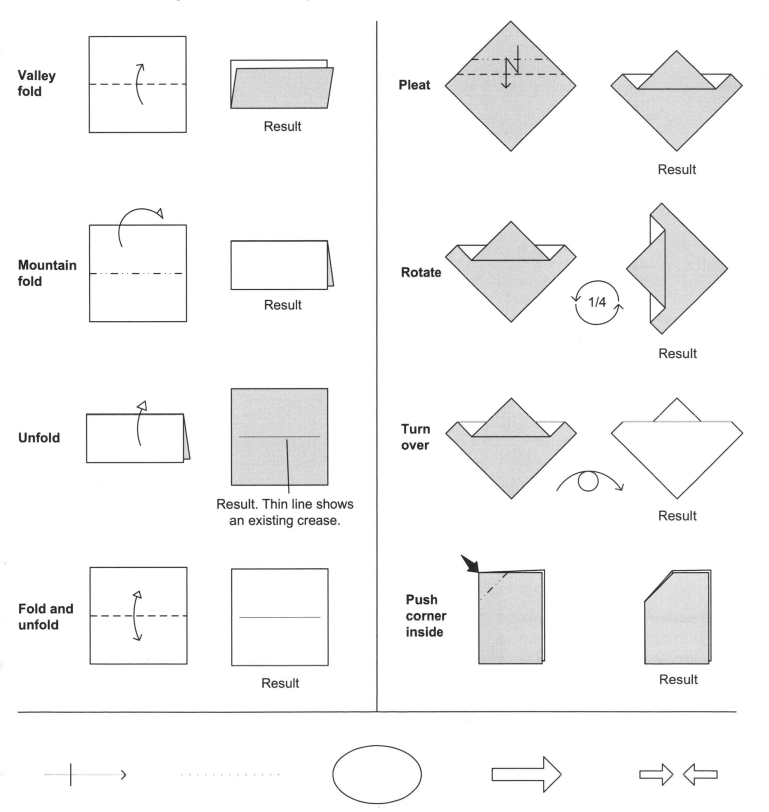

Valley fold

Result

Mountain fold

Result

Unfold

Result. Thin line shows an existing crease.

Fold and unfold

Result

Pleat

Result

Rotate

1/4

Result

Turn over

Result

Push corner inside

Result

Repeat steps on other flap

X-ray view or guideline

Enlarged detail view

Insert

Pinch

Section 1: Models with Mouths and Eyes that Open and Shut

The models in this section share these features:

➤ They're constructed from perpendicular cross-pleats.
➤ They fold up like a fan or accordion.

A pleat is the result of folding the paper back and forth such that one portion overlaps another; a cross-pleat is when you first pleat the paper in one direction (left-right), and then with those folds in place, you pleat the paper in the other direction (up-down).

The instructions at the beginning of this section detail how to crease the model into equal divisions; those at the end assume you know how to do this, so they simply indicate how many divisions to make.

A good practice is to fold all horizontal creases in both directions, that is, as valley- and mountain-folds. That way, it will be easier to make your pleats go either way in later steps. Also, the first time you make a model with many horizontal divisions, you may want to write the numbers on the creases to correspond to the numbers referred to in the directions.

Facial features, like a mouth or nose, are created by pulling out a horizontal pleat that lies within the "valley" between two vertical pleats, and recreasing it so that it juts out at an angle. This maneuver may prove to be a bit tricky at first. One way to get good results is to do the following:

1. Pull the paper out until it's in the right position.
2. Make light creases so that the pulled-out section stays pulled out.
3. Gently close up the model, but not all the way.
4. Open the model to make sure the creases are in the right place and adjust accordingly.
5. Finally, close up (fan-fold) the model firmly to set the creases.

One technique that might help is to close up all the vertical pleats of the model except for the single "valley" you're working in. This gives you more control.

Talking Bird

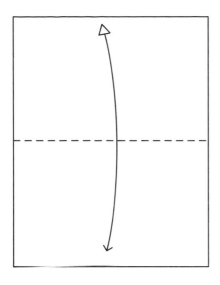

1. Valley-fold and unfold the top edge to the bottom.

2. Valley-fold the top and bottom edges to the center.

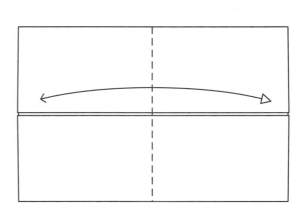

3. Valley-fold and unfold the right edge to the left.

4. Mountain-fold and unfold the left and right edges to the center. (Turn over and make valley-folds.)

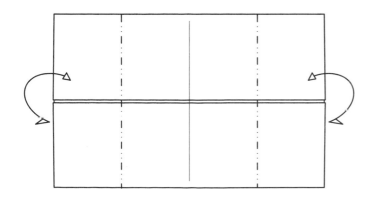

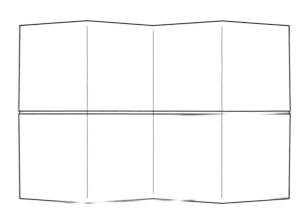

Here is the result. Continue with step 5 on the next page.

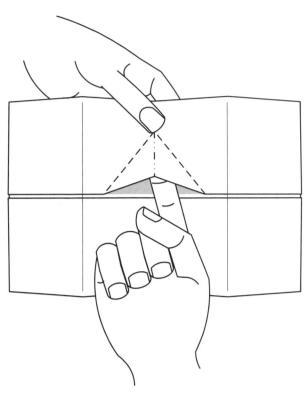

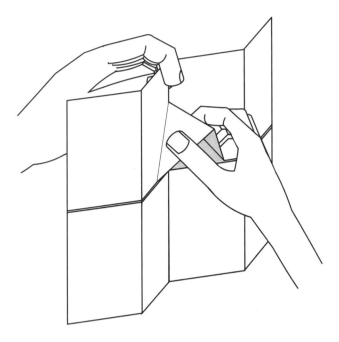

5. Lift out the top flap from the center slit into a beak, while holding down the top portion of the model. There are no landmarks for this move; you decide how big the beak will be. The valley- and mountain-fold lines on the diagram are suggestive only.

6. Pinch together the two sides of the beak.

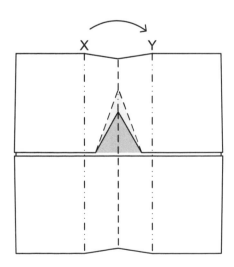

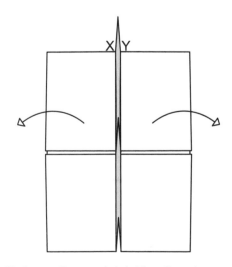

7. Shut the beak inside by pushing the left and right sides together, bringing crease X to crease Y.

8. Release the model, letting it spring open.

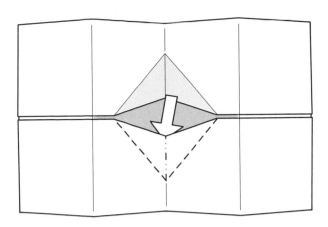

9. Repeat steps 5-8 on the bottom flap to make the lower beak.

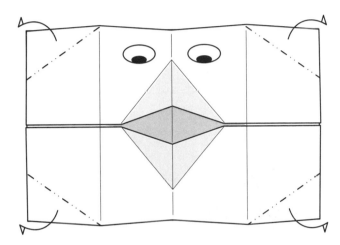

10. The top and bottom beaks are finished. Mountain-fold the four corners behind to shape the face. Draw eyes on if you like.

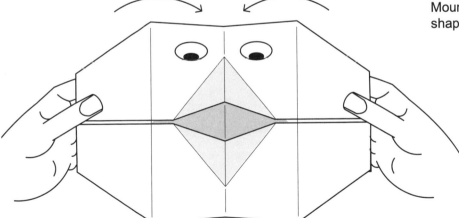

To make the bird talk, hold the left and right flaps and bring them together and apart.

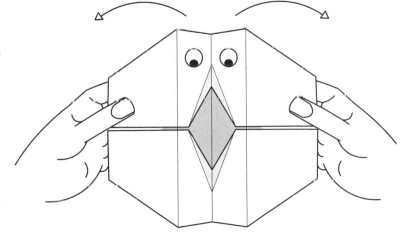

Masked Super Hero

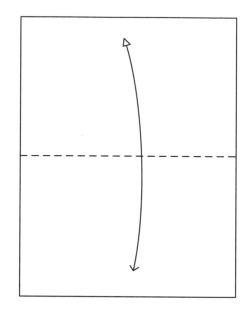

1. Valley-fold and unfold the top edge to the bottom.

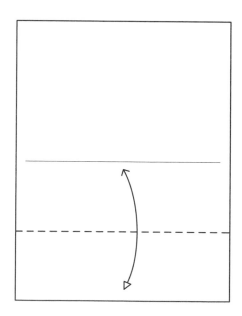

2. Valley-fold and unfold the bottom edge to the center.

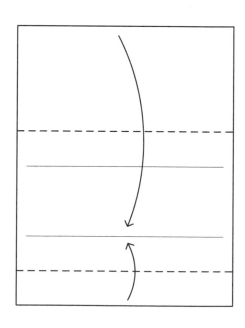

3. Valley-fold the top and bottom edges to the crease you made in step 2.

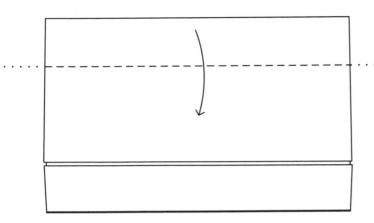

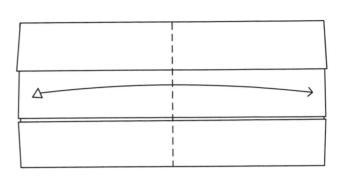

4. Valley-fold the model over along the existing crease from the rear flap. The dotted line indicates the location of this crease.

5. Valley-fold and unfold the left edge to the right.

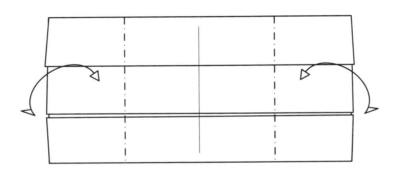

6. Mountain-fold and unfold the left and right edges to the center crease (made in step 5).

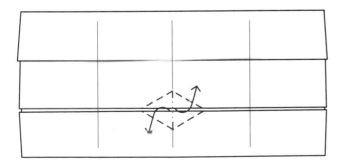

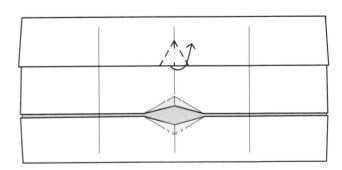

7. Form the mouth by lifting and creasing the flaps top and bottom as shown here. The placement of the creases is up to you; for a bigger mouth, lift further before creasing.

8. Form the nose by lifting and creasing the edge above the mouth. You can make the nose as big or as small as you want.

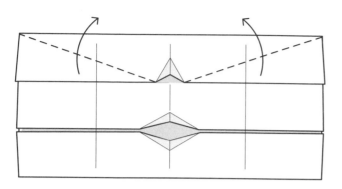

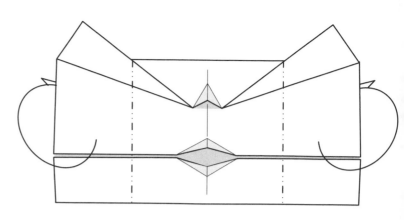

9. Valley-fold the lower corners of the top edge up, connecting the upper left and right corners with the points on the left and right base of the nose.

10. Mountain-fold the right and left sides behind along existing creases.

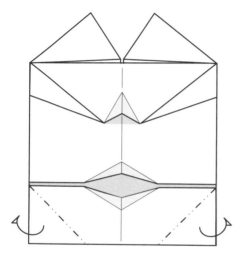

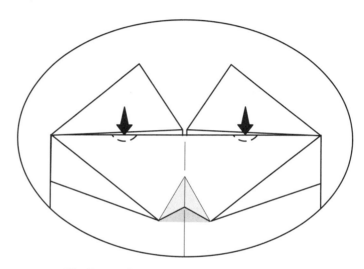

11. Shape the face by mountain-folding the lower left and right corners behind.

12. Create impressions of eyes by pushing downward into the horizontal edge near the top. Make these indentations only on the near edge.

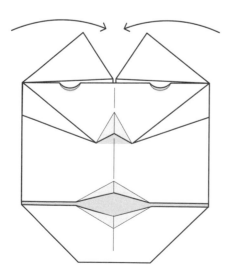

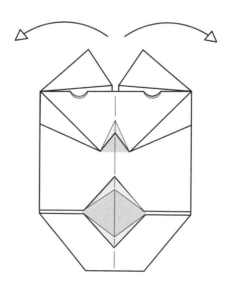

Here is the result. To make the model talk, open and close it like a book.

Blowfish

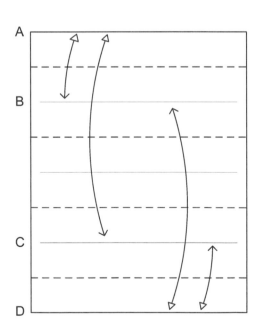

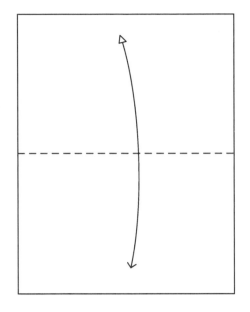

1. Valley-fold and unfold the top edge to the bottom.

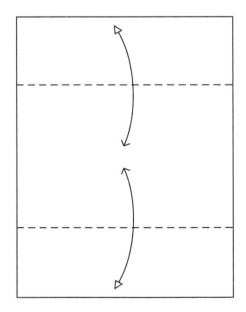

2. Valley-fold and unfold the top and bottom edges to the center.

3. Divide the paper into eighths —valley-fold and unfold A to B, A to C, D to C, D to B. Then reverse the directions of all seven creases, turning the valley folds into mountain folds. This will make it easier to make the pleats in the following steps.

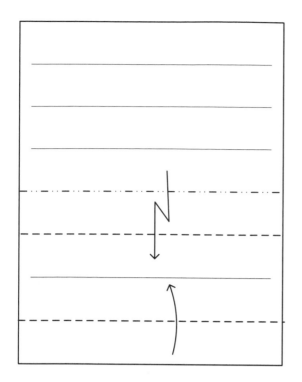

4. Valley-fold the bottom edge up to the second crease. Pleat the paper as shown.

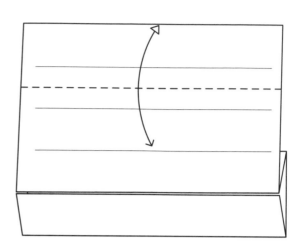

5. Valley-fold and unfold the top edge down to the 3rd crease from the top.

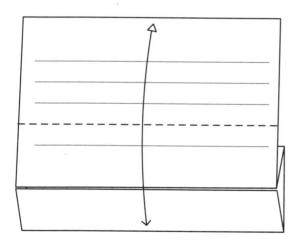

6. Valley-fold and unfold the top edge down to the bottom edge.

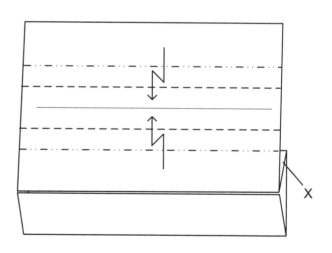

7. Make two sets of pleats as shown. Tuck the lower pleat <u>inside</u> the large pleat (X); do not wrap it over.

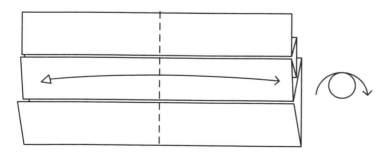

8. Valley-fold and unfold the model in half left to right. **Then turn the model over.**

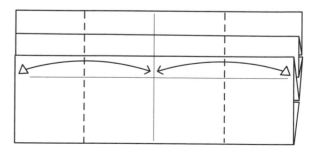

9. Valley-fold and unfold the two sides to the center.

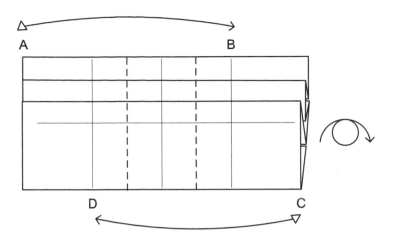

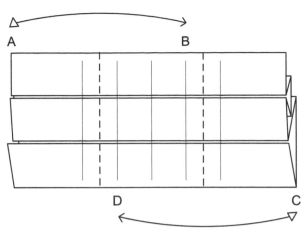

10. Valley-fold and unfold edge A to crease B, then edge C to crease D. **Then turn the model over.**

11. Valley-fold and unfold edge A to crease B, then edge C to crease D.

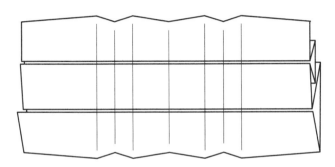

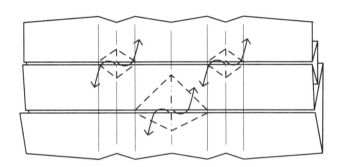

Here is the result of all the pleating.

12. Form the eyes and mouth with valley- and mountain-folds. The top portion of the mouth should be larger than the bottom. The exact placement of these creases is up to you. You may want to use a pointed object, like a blunt pen, to open up these areas.

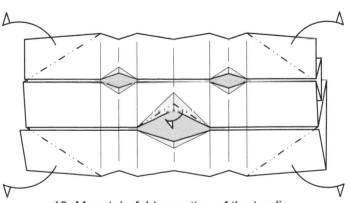

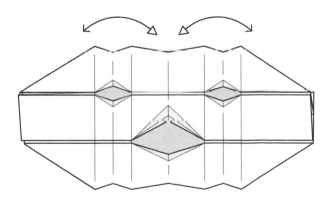

13. Mountain-fold a portion of the top lip under. Mountain-fold all four corners behind to shape the face.

To make the blowfish talk and blink, pull the model apart and push it together.

Singer

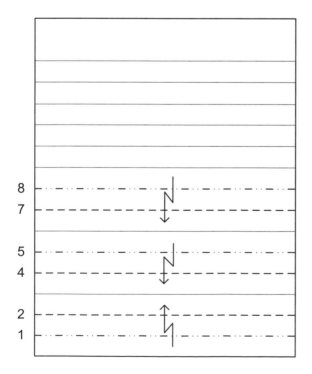

1. Divide the paper into 8 equal sections, then divide each of those sections in half, except for the top one. Fold each crease in both directions (valley and mountain) to make it easier to make your pleats in later steps.

2. Make the mountain- and valley-folds indicated to form three pleats. The crease numbers refer to their order from the bottom of the paper.

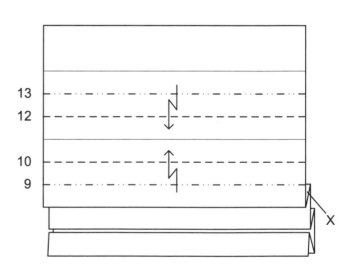

3. Make two sets of pleats as shown. Wrap the lower pleat outside the large pleat (X).

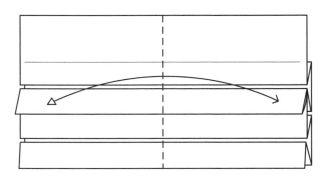

4. Valley-fold and unfold the model in half left to right.

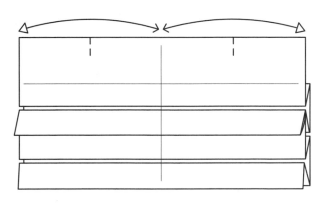

5. Bring the left and right edges to the center and make pinch-marks. Then unfold.

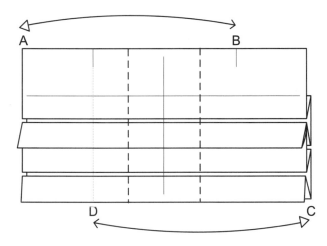

6. Valley-fold and unfold edge A to pinch-mark B, then edge C to pinch-mark D.

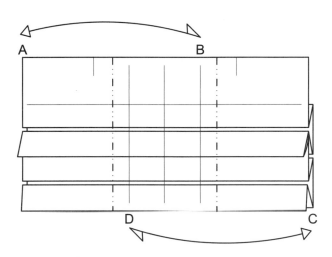

7. Mountain-fold and unfold edge A to crease B, then edge C to crease D.

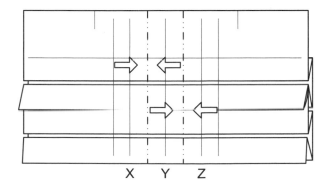

8. Make the indicated mountain-folds. An easy way to do this is by creating ridges by bringing together creases X and Y, and Z and Y. The arrows indicate the areas to be pinched.

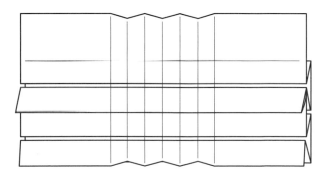

Here is the result. Continue with step 9.

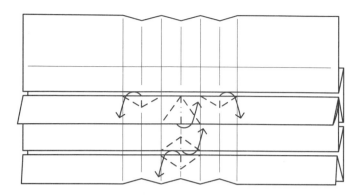

9. Form the eyes, nose, and mouth with valley- and mountain-folds. You may want to use a pointed object, like a blunt pen, to open up these areas.

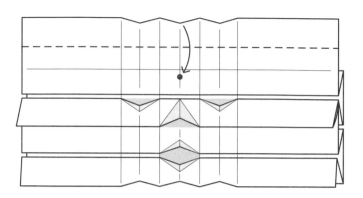

10. Valley-fold the top edge down to just below the existing crease, indicated with a dot. The lower you go, the closer the eyebrows will be to the eyes.

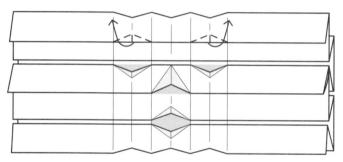

11. Create impressions of eyebrows by making the indicated valley- and mountain-folds. Then unfold.

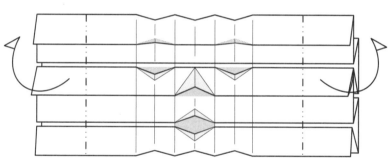

12. Mountain-fold the sides to first creases on either side.

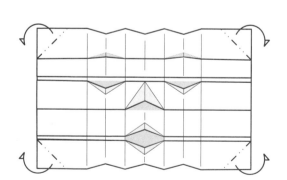

13. Mountain-fold all four corners behind to shape the face.

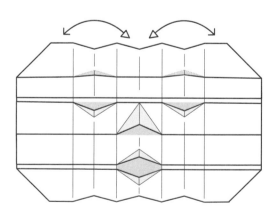

To make the singer sing, pull the model apart and push it together.

Choir

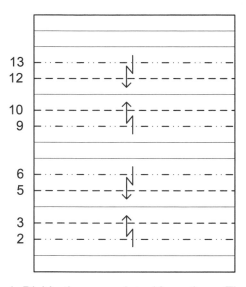

1. Divide the paper into 16 sections. Then make the mountain- and valley-folds indicated to form four pleats. The crease numbers indicate their order from the bottom of the paper.

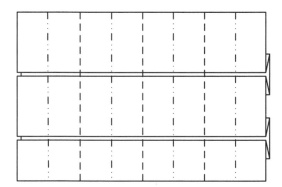

2. Divide the model into 8 vertical sections with alternating mountain- and valley-folds.

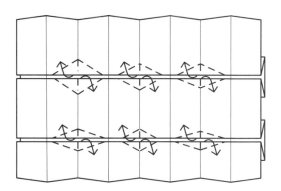

3. Form the mouths of the six singers by pulling open the flaps and making the indicated creases. They should be of different sizes.

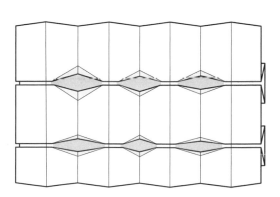

Here is the result.

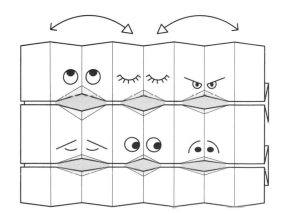

Draw different kinds of eyes to reflect the different singers' personalities. To make the choir sing, push and pull the model together and apart.

African Mask

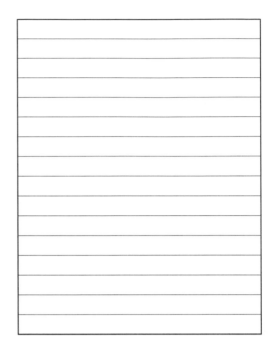

1. Divide the paper into 16 equal sections. Fold each crease in both directions (valley and mountain) to make it easier to make your pleats in later steps.

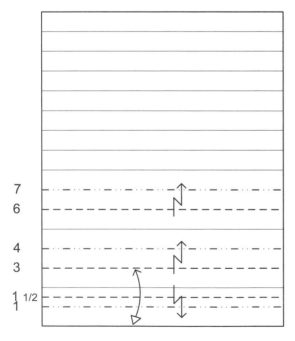

2. First make crease 1 1/2 by folding and unfolding the bottom edge to crease 3. Then make the other indicated mountain- and valley-folds. The numbers refer to the order from the bottom.

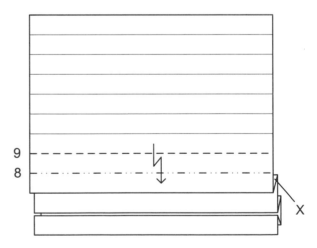

3. Make the indicated pleat, tucking valley-fold 9 entirely <u>inside</u> pleat X.

20

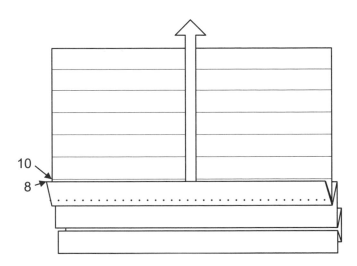

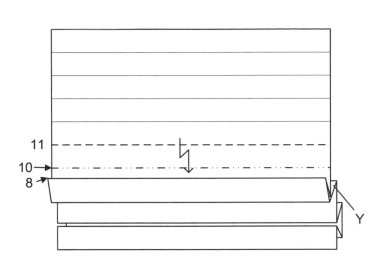

4. Slide the top portion of the model up just a little from within the pleat you made in step 3, and then flatten. A new valley fold will be created inside, indicated by the dotted line. When finished, crease 10 will be repositioned about 1/4 inch above crease 8.

5. Make the indicated pleat, tucking valley-fold 11 entirely <u>inside</u> pleat Y.

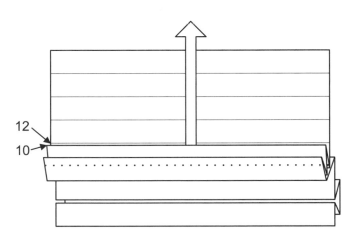

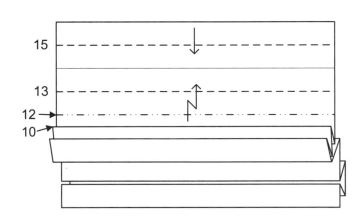

6. Slide the top portion of the model up just a little from within the pleat you made in step 5, and then flatten. A new valley fold will be created inside, indicated by the dotted line. When finished, crease 12 will be repositioned about 1/4 inch above crease 10.

7. Make a pleat along creases 12 and 13, and valley-fold at 15.

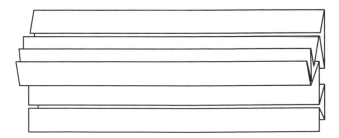

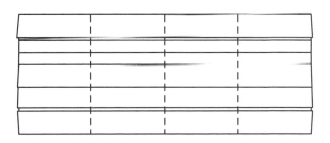

Here's the result of all the pleating, shown in perspective so you can see how the pleats are arranged. From here on, the diagrams will show the model from the front.

8. Divide the model vertically into quarters with valley folds.

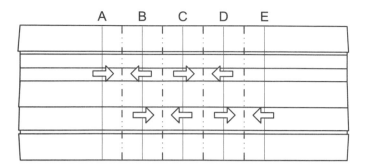

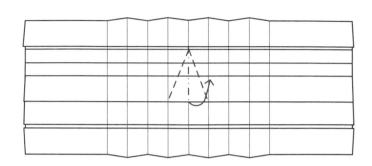

8. Divide each of the four center sections in half with mountain folds. One way to do this is to create ridges by bringing together creases A to B, B to C, C to D, and D to E. The arrows indicate the areas to be pinched.

9. In this step you'll make the nose. Since the nose crosses multiple pleats, you'll have to first pre-crease through all thicknesses of the model with valley folds as indicated. Then, working from the back of the model, push the nose outward along the crease lines. Some of the pleats may get crumpled a little on the inside from this move, but they won't show from the front.

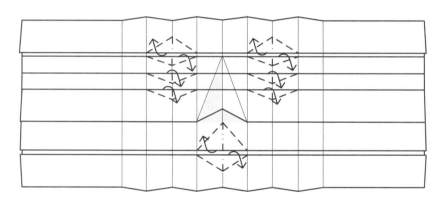

10. Form the eyes, creases under the eyes, and mouth with valley- and mountain-folds.

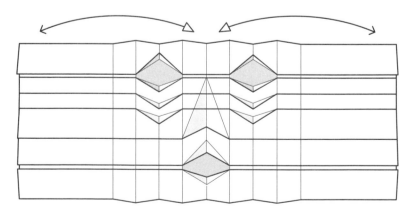

To make the African mask talk, pull the model apart and push it together.

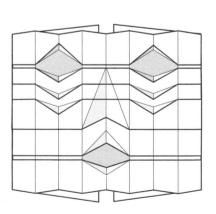

You can also fold the left and right side flaps behind to show just the mask.

Section 2: Models with Jaws that Snap and Ears that Pop Out

The animal faces in this section all have pop-up snouts, and ears that protrude either from the top or the side of the head. With most of the models, you draw in the eyes when the folding is done; with some models, the eyes emerge as a result of folding—the baboon's eyes are suggested by a pleat, and the wolf's eyes appear when the model is held up to a light.

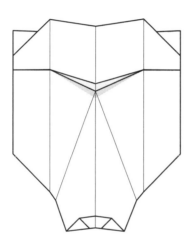 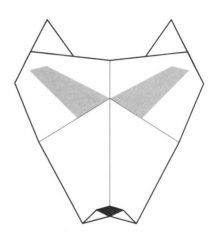

As I was designing these models, I learned through trial and error that the angle at which the snout pops out can be critical in conveying the essence of the animal. With the monkey, for example, if I sharpened or broadened the angle of the snout, or moved it the tiniest bit, the model lost some of its monkey-like traits.

That's why I tried as much as possible to use landmarks and reference points in the folding sequences—to help ensure that your results would match those in the book. If your model doesn't look like its subject, then the angle of the snout is one of the first things to check.

Elephant

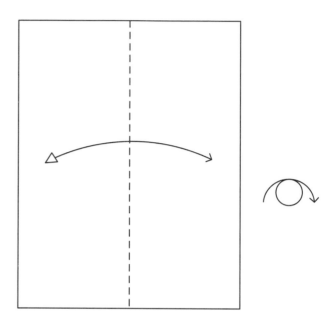

1. Valley-fold and unfold
   the left edge to the right.
   Turn the model over.

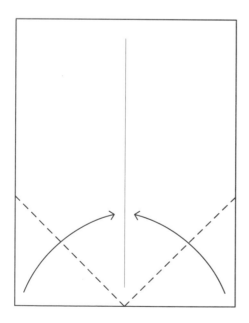

2. Valley-fold the lower left and right
   corners to the center crease.

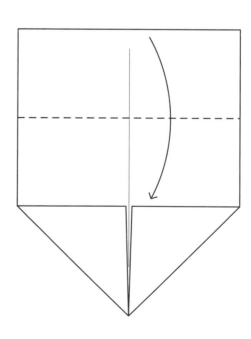

3. Valley-fold the top edge to the
   top edges of the triangular flaps.

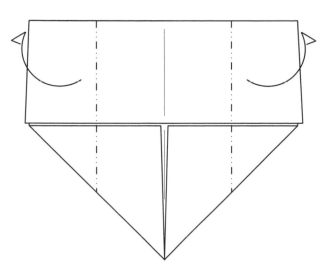

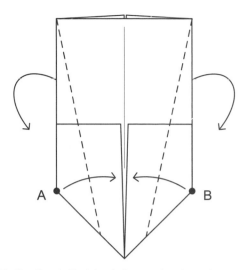

4. Mountain-fold the left and right edges to the center.

5. On the left side, bring point A to the center, allowing the rear flap to swing out to the side, then valley-fold. Do the same thing on the right side with point B.

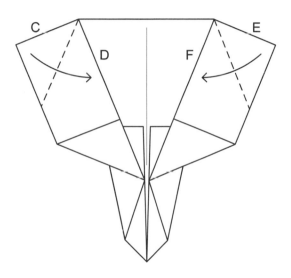

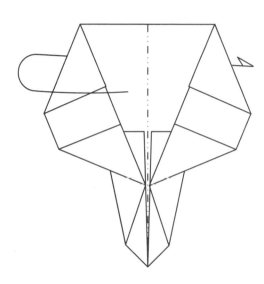

6. Valley-fold the upper left and right corners inward, edge C to D, and E to F.

7. Mountain-fold the model in half, swinging the left side behind to the right.

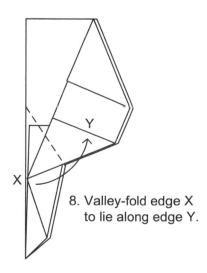

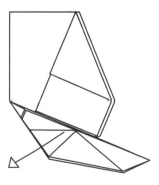

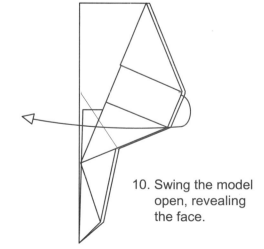

8. Valley-fold edge X to lie along edge Y.

9. Unfold step 8.

10. Swing the model open, revealing the face.

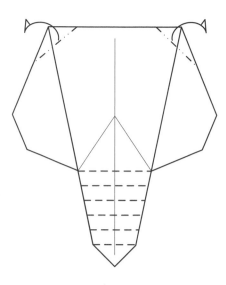

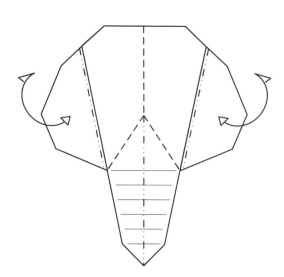

11. Shape the top of the head as you like with mountain folds. (If you want to make them even, fold one corner, then fold the model in half again and match the crease.) Make valley creases along the trunk, spacing them as desired.

12. Mountain-fold the ear flaps behind, then unfold. To bring the face into 3-D, make the indicated valley- and mountain-folds along existing creases.

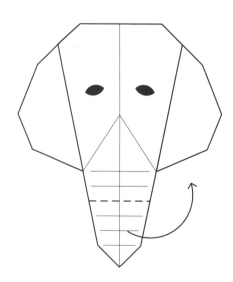

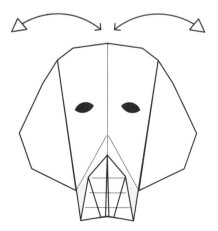

To make the elephant lift and lower his trunk, hold the model by the ears and bring your hands together and apart.

13. Draw eyes in if you like. Valley-fold the trunk up at one of the creases you made in step 11. (It doesn't matter which one.)

Panda or Bear

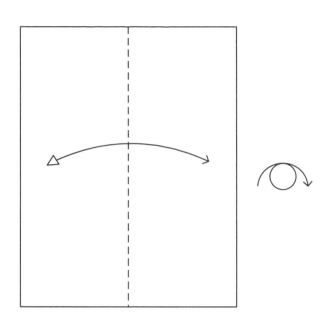

1. Valley-fold and unfold the left edge to the right. **Turn the model over.**

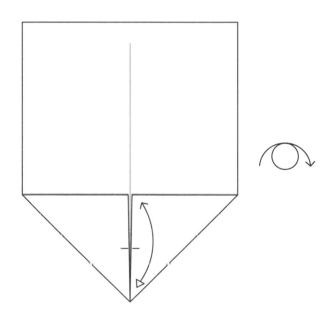

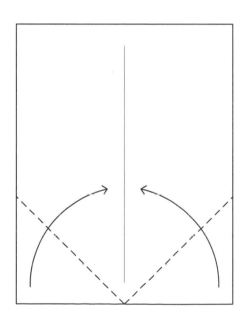

2. Valley-fold the two lower corners to the middle crease.

3. Make a pinch mark (fold and unfold) at the half-way point between the bottom point and the top edges of the triangular flaps. **Turn the model over.**

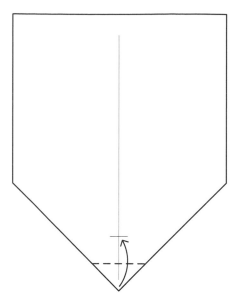

4. Valley-fold the bottom point to the pinch mark you made in step 3.

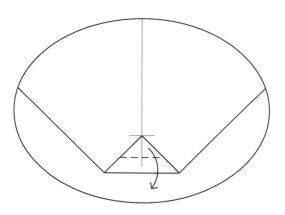

5. Valley-fold the tip of the triangular flap downward so that it extends a little beyond the bottom of the model.

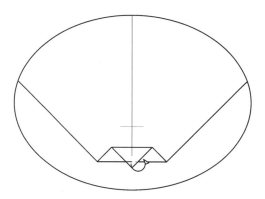

6. Mountain-fold the part of the triangle that extends beyond the model under the top layer.

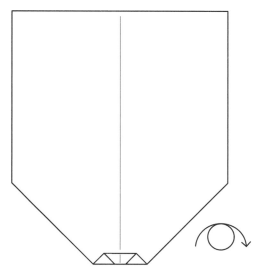

7. Here is the result. **Turn the model over.**

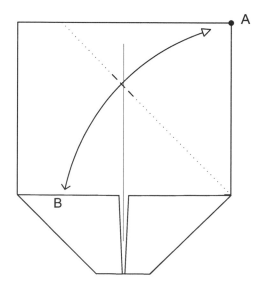

8. Bring point A down until it lies along edge B, but don't crease all the way — just make a pinch mark where the diagonal crease intersects the vertical center crease.

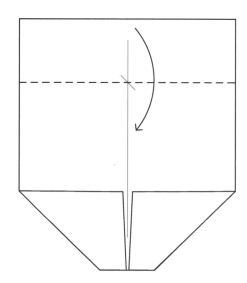

9. Valley-fold the top of the model at the intersection mark you made in step 8.

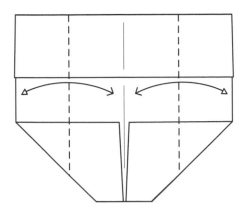

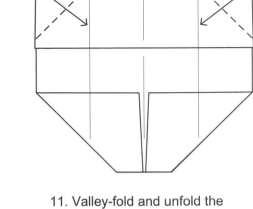

10. Valley-fold and unfold the sides to the center.

11. Valley-fold and unfold the upper right and left corners to the indicated creases.

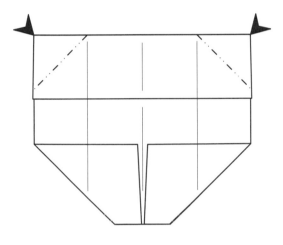

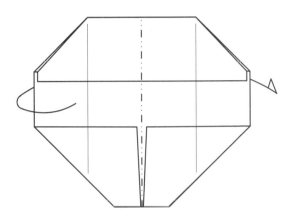

12. Push the corners inside along the creases you made in step 11. This move is called an "inside reverse-fold."

13. Mountain-fold the model in half, swinging the left side behind to the right.

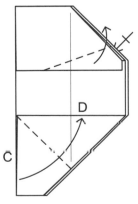

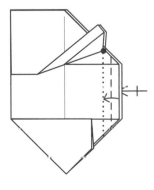

14. To make the ear, valley-fold the top flap so that it extends out beyond the model. Only go as far as the paper underneath allows you to. (See the next step.) Repeat this behind so that the positions of the ear flaps match. Valley-fold edge C to edge D.

15. Valley-fold the right edge to the dotted line, which extends down from the dot. Repeat behind.

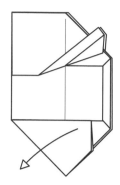

16. Unfold the last crease made in step 14.

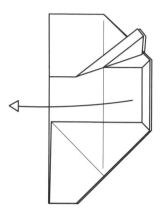

17. Swing the model open, revealing the face.

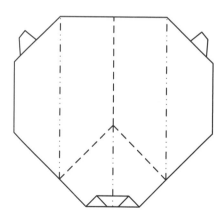

18. To bring the face into 3-D, make the indicated valley- and mountain-folds along existing creases.

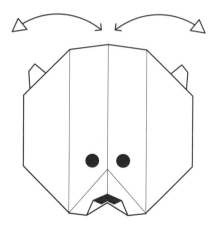

To make the bear talk, hold the left and right flaps and bring them together. The snout will move up and down.

The markings on this drawing indicate a bear. With different eye markings and colored-in ears, you'll have a panda. (See the first page of this set of diagrams.)

Dog

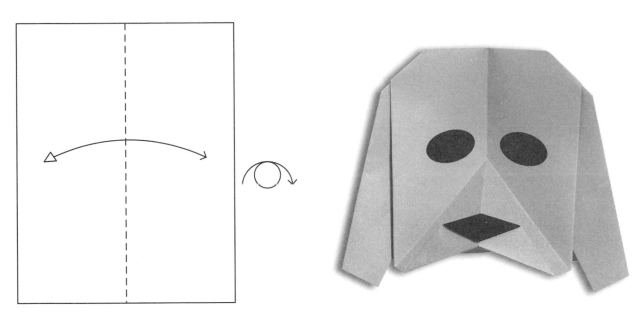

1. Valley-fold and unfold the left edge to the right. **Then turn the model over.**

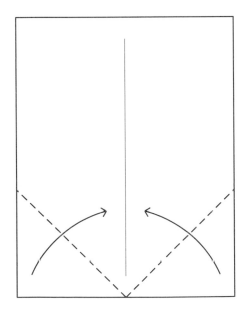

2. Valley-fold the two lower corners to the middle crease.

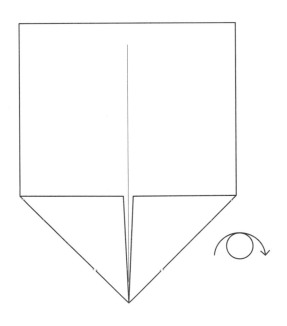

3. **Turn the model over.**

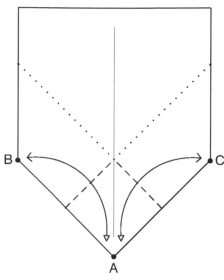

4. Valley-fold and unfold point A to point B, but only crease to the center. The dotted lines show where the fold would have extended. Repeat by folding and unfolding point A to point C.

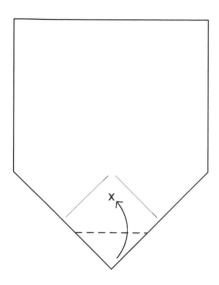

5. Valley-fold the bottom point up to the "x," which is about 1/2 inch below the intersection of the two creases made in step 4.

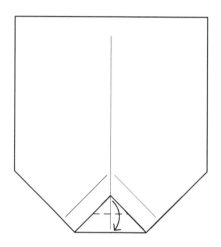

6. Valley-fold the point of the triangle to meet the bottom edge.

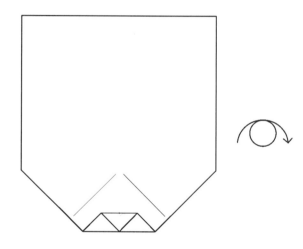

7. **Turn the model over.**

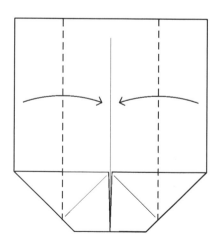

8. Valley-fold the two sides to the center.

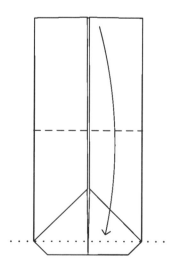

9. Valley-fold the top edge down to the bottom of the rectangular area, indicated with a dotted line.

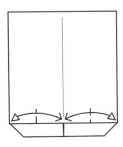
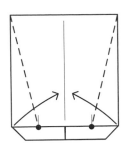
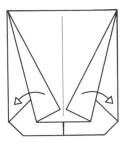

10. Valley-fold and unfold the right and left edges to the center (top layer only), but just make pinch-marks.

11. Make valley creases that connect the upper left and right corners to end points of the pinch-marks made in the previous step, indicated with dots.

12. Unfold step 11.

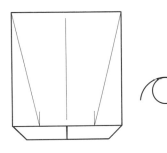
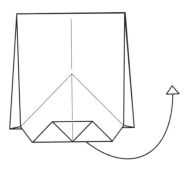

13. **Turn the model over.**

14. Unfold the model along the center horizontal crease.

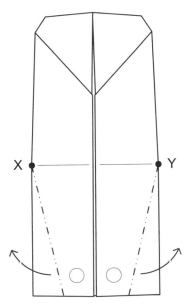
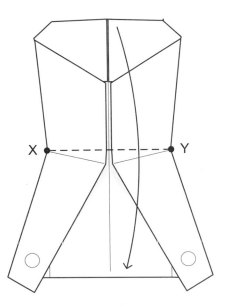

15a. Slide the top layers outward from points X and Y, along the creases you made in step 11. As you do this, the top flap will curl toward you. The hollow circles indicate the portions of the flaps that will remain visible once the move is completed.

15b. In process. Notice the position of the two circles. Continue folding the top down along XY until the model lies flat.

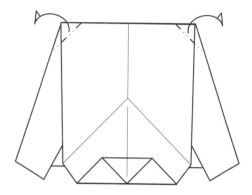

16. Shape the top of the head as you like with mountain folds. (If you want to make them even, fold one corner, then fold the model in half again and match the crease.)

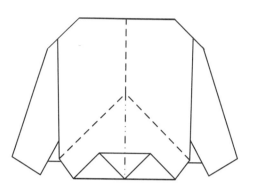

17. Make the indicated mountain- and valley-folds along existing creases. The snout will pop out.

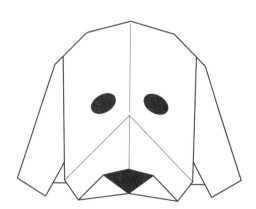

18. Here is the result. Draw eyes on and color the nose if you like.

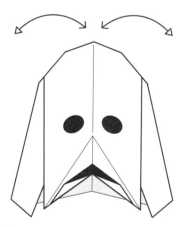

To make the dog talk, open and close the model like a book. The snout will move up and down.

Baboon

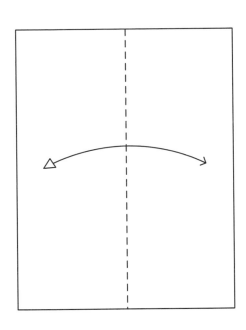

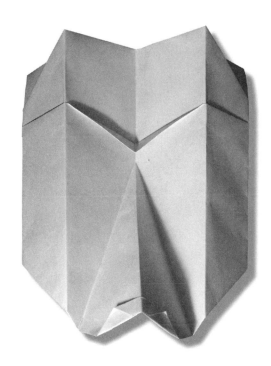

1. Valley-fold and unfold the
   left edge to the right. **Then
   turn the model over.**

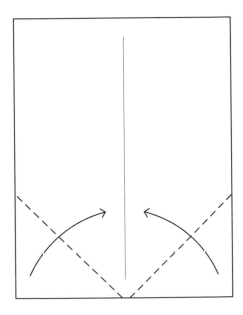

2. Valley-fold the two lower corners
   to the middle crease. However,
   don't start the creases exactly at
   the center; leave a little gap.

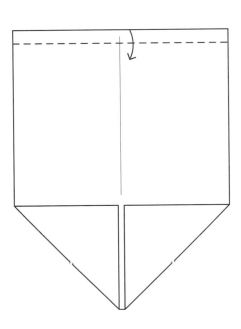

3. Valley-fold the top edge
   down about 1/2 inch.

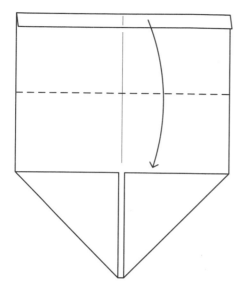

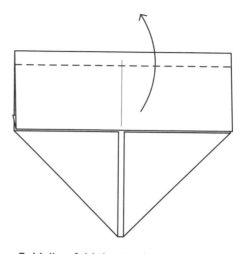

4. Valley-fold the top folded edge down to the top edges of the triangular flaps.

5. Valley-fold the top layer back up, leaving a pleat of about 1/2 inch.

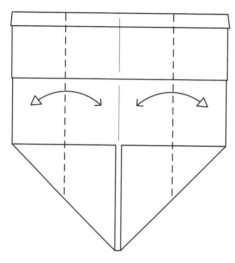

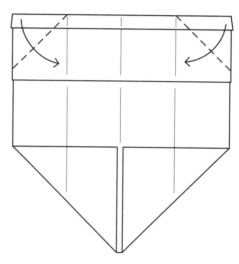

6. Valley-fold and unfold the right and left edges to the center.

7. Valley-fold the upper right and left corners so that the edges lie along the nearest vertical creases.

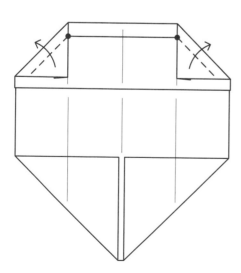

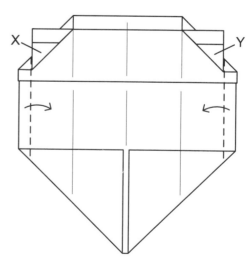

8. Valley-fold the corners created in step 7 back out, starting at the black dots.

9. Valley-fold the two sides in right and left so that they cover the lower corners of flaps X and Y.

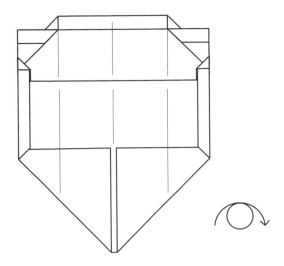

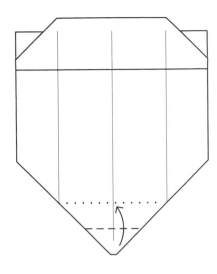

10. **Turn the model over.**

10. Valley-fold the bottom point up to where the vertical creases meet the edges of the model. A dotted line shows where this is.

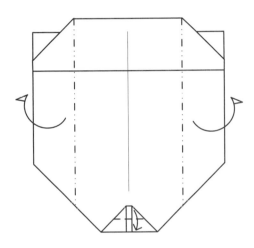

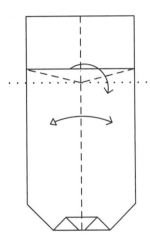

11. Valley-fold the tip of the triangular flap down to meet the bottom edge. Then mountain-fold the two sides behind along existing creases.

12. In this step you make the eyes. Valley-fold diagonally along the pleated area. After making these two creases, pull the pleat down. As you do, valley-fold the model in half vertically, then unfold.

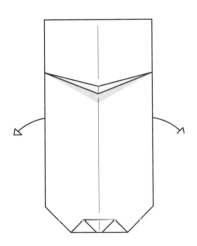

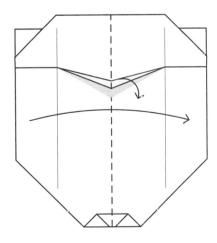

13. Unfold the two side flaps,

14. Valley-fold the model in half left to right, while tipping the eye flap downward.

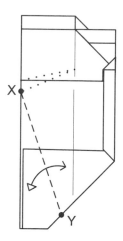

15. Valley-fold and unfold the lower portion of the model up and to the right. Point X is the bottom of the diagonal flap created in step 12, now inside the model, indicated by the dotted line. Point Y lies along the bottom of the diagonal edge. (There is no reference for point Y.)

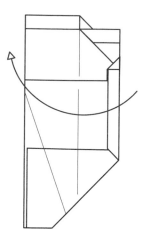

16. Swing the model open, revealing the face.

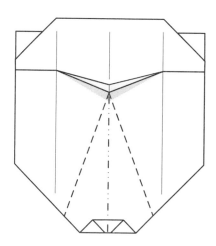

17. Make the valley-folds along the creases made in step 15. Then mountain-fold along the center from under the eyes down to the bottom. This makes the baboon's snout come out in 3-D.

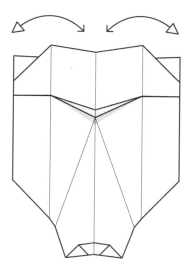

To make the baboon talk, hold the left and right flaps and bring them together and apart. The eyes will move and the snout will go up and down.

Wolf

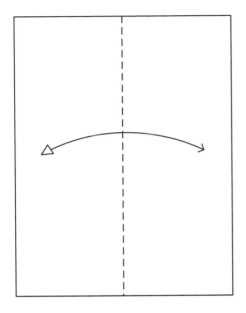

1. Valley-fold and unfold the left edge to the right.

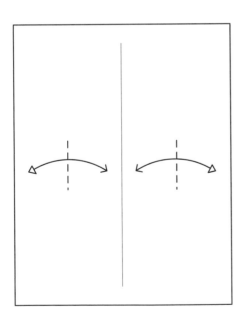

2. Valley-fold and unfold the left and right edges to the center crease, but only make pinch marks. Do not crease all the way.

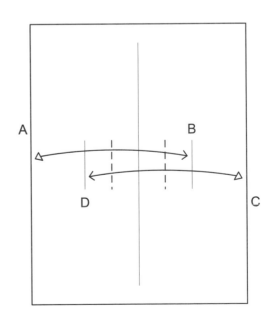

3. Valley-fold and unfold edge A to crease B and make a pinch mark. Valley-fold and unfold edge C to crease D and make a pinch mark.

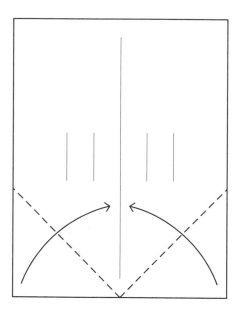

4. Valley-fold the lower left and right corners to the center crease.

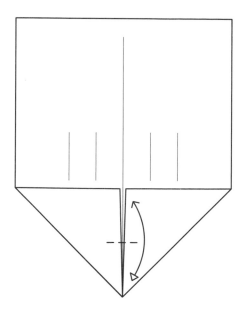

5. Valley-fold and unfold the bottom point to where the corners of the triangles meet in the center. Make a pinch mark. Do not crease all the way across.

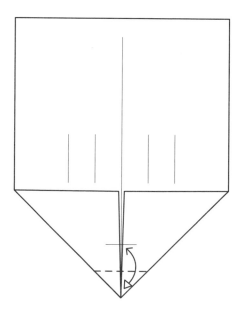

6. Valley-fold and unfold the bottom point to the crease made in step 5.

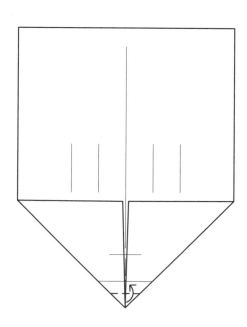

7. Valley-fold the bottom point to the crease made in step 6.

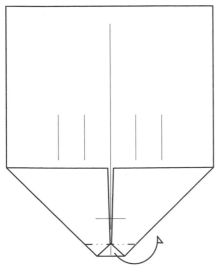

8. Reverse the direction of the valley-fold made in step 6, changing it to a mountain-fold.

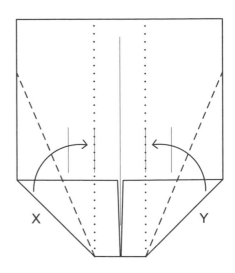

9. Valley-fold edges X and Y to the guide creases made in step 3. The dotted lines show how these edges are to line up.

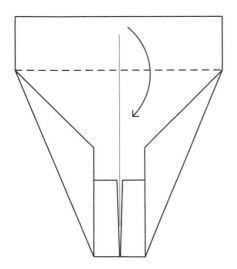

10. Valley-fold the top edge down.

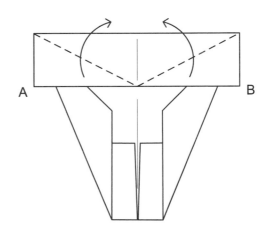

11. Valley-fold corners A and B up along the diagonals.

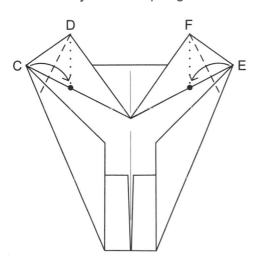

12. Valley-fold corners C and E to the dots, which are directly below corners D and F. The dotted lines show the position of edges CD and EF.

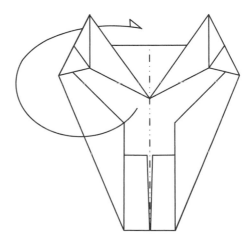

13. Mountain-fold the entire model in half vertically, swinging the left edge behind all the way to the right.

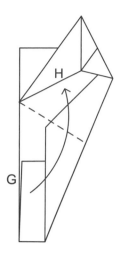

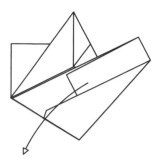

15. Unfold step 14.

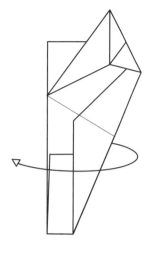

14. Valley-fold edge G to lie along edge H.

16. Swing the model open, revealing the face.

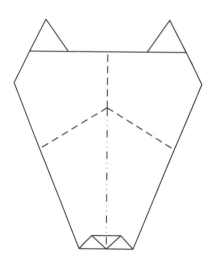

17. Make the valley-folds along the crease made in step 14. Then mountain-fold along the center from where those folds meet down to the bottom. This makes the wolf's snout come out in 3-D.

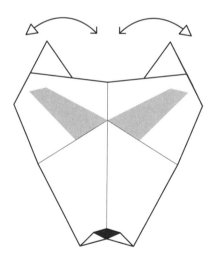

Here is the result. You can color the tip of the nose if you like. If you hold the model up to the light, eyes appear as shown by the gray areas.

To make the wolf talk, hold the model on both sides of the head above the snout, and bring your hands together and apart.

Monkey

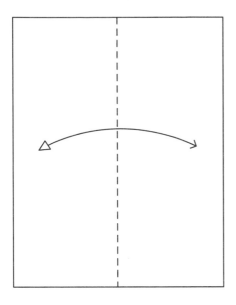

1. Valley-fold and unfold
   the left edge to the right.

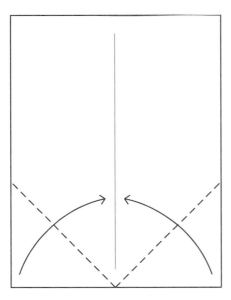

2. Valley-fold the lower left and right
   corners to the center crease.

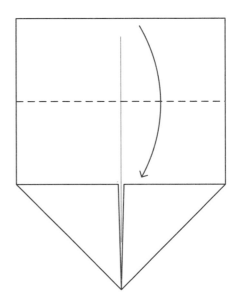

3. Valley-fold the top edge to the
   top edges of the triangular flaps.

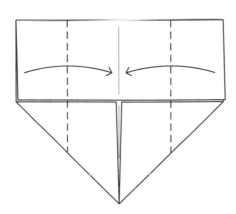

4. Valley-fold the left and
   right edges to the center.

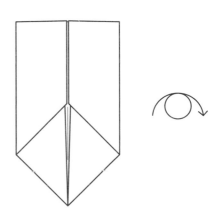

5. Here is the result.
   Turn the model over.

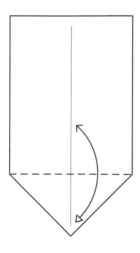

6. Valley-fold and unfold the bottom triangular point.

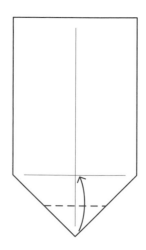

7. Valley-fold the bottom triangular point up to the crease made in step 6.

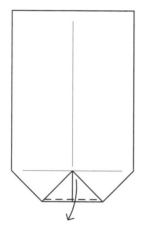

8. Valley-fold the triangular flap back down, leaving a little pleat.

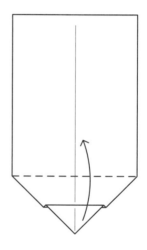

9. Restore the crease made in step 6.

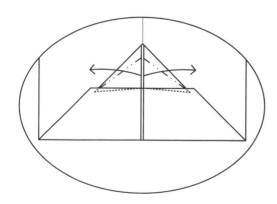

10. To create a snout, spread apart the triangular flap on both sides and re-crease along the indicated mountain folds. Beneath the pleat, the valley-folds (shown with dotted lines) are produced automatically.

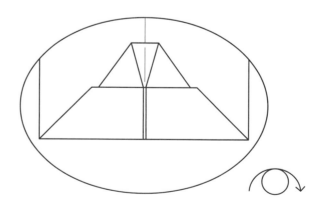

11. Here is the result. **Turn the model over.**

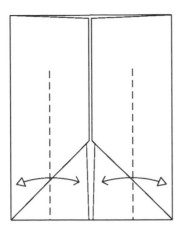

12. Valley-fold and unfold the left and right edges to the center, but only three-fourths of the way up.

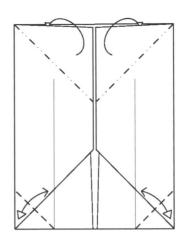

13. Mountain-fold the corners at the top of the model inside. Valley-fold the lower left and right corners to the creases you made In step 12, then unfold.

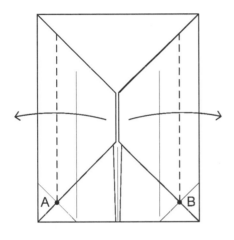

14. Valley-fold the flaps outward beginning at points A and B.

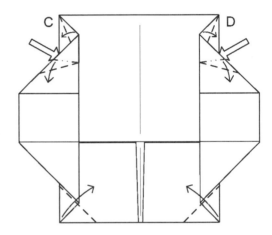

15. Valley-fold flaps C and D in half, and at the same time, swivel-fold the paper on top downward into pleats. See the next step for the result. Valley fold the lower left and right corners up along existing creases.

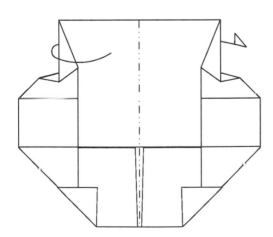

16. Mountain-fold the model In half, swinging the left side around behind to the right.

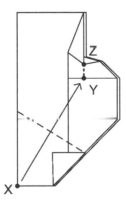

17. Valley-fold point X to meet point Y, which is directly below point Z.

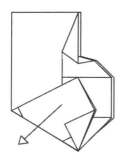

18. Unfold step 17.

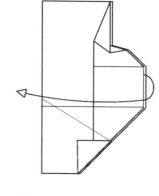

19. Swing the model open,
    revealing the face.

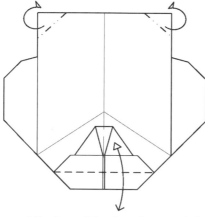

20. To round the top of the head, mountain-fold the
    top corners behind at any angle you like. (If you
    want to make them even, fold one corner, then
    fold the model in half again and match the
    crease.) Valley-fold the mouth and nose structure
    down at the widest point, then unfold.

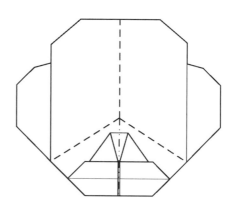

21. To bring the face into 3-D, make the
    indicated valley- and mountain-folds
    along existing creases.

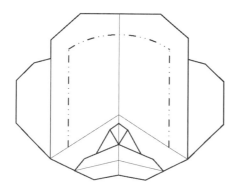

22. Add further definition to the face
    with mountain-creases.

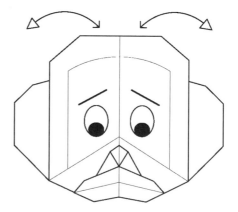

Here is the result. You can draw in eyes and
eyebrows if you like.

To make the monkey talk, hold the model at the
ears, and bring your hands together and apart.

Tips for Creating Your Own Models

Section 1: Models with Mouths and Eyes that Open and Shut

The models in section 1 were all designed with evenly spaced perpendicular creases, because they're easy to work with when you're first starting out. The variations described here, however, encourage you to move beyond these design restrictions.

A simple variation is the following: Once you've completed a model, prepare another one using the same grid, then turn it over or upside-down. From a different perspective, the same cross-pleated grid can yield a very different result!

Here's another idea. Don't space your horizontal mountain and valley folds at regular intervals, like eighths or sixteenths. Instead, space them at arbitrary intervals, sometimes leaving gaps between pleats, sometimes overlapping them. Once the grid is established, tease out "eye," "nose," and "mouth" flaps at random. See what kinds of faces suggest themselves to you—they don't have to be symmetrical.

Also, try sloping your vertical creases diagonally from the top—like a pyramid—instead of making them perpendicular. This technique produces eyes that are close together and have an interesting tilt.

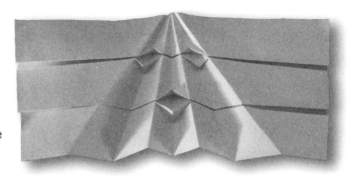

Finally, don't feel restricted to having only one face as your subject. As with the "Choir" (page 19), more than one face can be portrayed within a single model.

Section 2: Models with Jaws that Snap and Ears that Pop Out

To make your own animal faces, find different pictures of your chosen subject and notice what features make them instantly recognizable. This isn't always obvious. For example, some types of pigs have ears pointing up, and some pointing down. You have to decide which type best conveys your subject.

Next, make a simple sketch of the animal to help you pinpoint the key features you'll want to use in your model.

Finally, see if any models in this book can serve as a base, and can be adapted for your purposes. For example, after looking at a number of pictures of foxes, you might decide that the most recognizable parts of a fox's face are its long, skinny snout, pointy ears, and triangular nose.

Looking through this book, you notice that the fox shares many features of the wolf (page 39)—mainly the shape of the head and the ears. The major difference is that the fox has a skinnier snout. So to make a fox, you could start off with the wolf, and then fold the edges of the snout closer into the center to make a skinnier version. (See left.)

Many mammals have noses shaped like a blunted triangle. In this book, you'll notice that the dog, bear, and wolf models all use a similar procedure for folding the nose. If you want to design a model with a similar nose—like a sheep, cat, or deer, for example—you could use steps 1-7 of the bear as a starting point. (See right.)

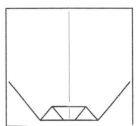

You might even take one feature and use it for a different purpose. For example, a crocodile has a long snout with eyes that stick out above the head. Starting with the wolf, you could alter the position and angle of the snout, then use the wolf's ears for the crocodile's eyes.

As you experiment, you'll discover many ways to mix and match features. You might even invent your own species!

Additional Resources

Books

There are hundreds of origami books available in many different languages. Here are a few in English geared toward beginning folders:

- *Origami Toys* by Florence Temko, Tuttle Publishing

- *Minigami: Mini Origami Projects for Cards, Gifts and Decorations* by Gay Merrill Gross, Firefly Books

- *Teach Yourself Origami* by John Montroll, Dover Publications

Paper

You can find origami paper at most art supply stores. Here are two sources on the web:

- *Origami-USA*
  www.origami-usa.org

- *Kim's Crane*
  www.kimscrane.com

These sources also carry origami books.

Organizations

Below are the two largest origami organizations in the English-speaking world. On their web sites you'll find lots of information, including listings of local area groups.

- *Origami-USA*
  www.origami-usa.org

- *British Origami Society*
  www.britishorigami.info

Web Sites

You can find just about anything you want to know about origami on the Internet. Here are some of the most popular and useful sites:

- *Wikipedia*
  en.wikipedia.org/wiki/Origami
  A great place to begin your exploration of origami.

- *Joseph Wu Origami*
  www.origami.as
  A rich catalog of origami information, including profiles of prominent folders and links to other sites.

- *Origami Swami*
  www.geocities.com/foldingca/swami.html
  A set of links to models from around the world, maintained by Dorothy Engleman. Excellent for beginners.

- *Origami Database*
  www.origamidatabase.com
  A comprehensive directory of origami models, searchable by model, designer, and book title, managed by Dennis Walker.

- *Gilad Aharoni's Web Site*
  www.giladorigami.com
  Reviews of many new origami books and journals.

Online Communities

There are several listservs for origami, and this is the oldest one, going back to 1988:

Origami-L Listserv
lists.digitalorigami.com/mailman/listinfo/origami

About the Author

Joel Stern has enjoyed origami since his childhood. A native of Omaha, Nebraska, he has conducted many origami workshops for all ages in camps, schools, community centers, and libraries. Joel is also the author of *Jewish Holiday Origami*, as well as *Washington Pops!*, a collection of do-it-yourself pop-up cards of famous buildings in Washington, D.C. His origami and pop-up creations have been exhibited in the U.S., Japan, and Israel. Joel lives in Los Angeles with his wife Susan and their three children. He can be reached at info@joeldstern.com.